MW01130268

SLOW COOKER DOG FOOD COOKBOOK

Dr. Doris Meany

SLOW COOKER DOG FOOD COOKBOOK

Disclaimer:

The content within this book is offered solely for general information purposes. The author and publisher disclaim any responsibility for actions taken in reliance on the material herein. Although every endeavor has been made to ensure the accuracy and comprehensiveness of the information, the author and publisher do not provide any explicit or implied guarantees regarding the reliability, appropriateness, or accessibility of the content contained in this book.

OTHER BOOKS BY THE AUTHOR

Homemade Dog Treats Using Baking Mats

Homemade Dog Biscuit Cookbook

IF YOU WOULD LIKE TO CHECK OUT MORE BOOKS BY DR.DORIS MEANY, SCAN THE QR CODE BELOW

TABLE OF CONTENTS

INTRODUCTION

In the heart of every dog lover lies a desire, an unspoken promise, a sacred bond woven in the tapestry of shared moments and unwavering loyalty. It's a story that begins not with words, but with a pulsating rhythm—paws dancing, tails wagging, and eyes twinkling with anticipation. For me, that story began with a silent vow to provide the best for my furry companion, a promise that sparked an odyssey that would change not just my life, but the lives of countless dog owners around the world.

Twenty years as a veterinary dietitian had gifted me the wisdom to understand the intricacies of canine nutrition, yet it was a moment of sheer desperation that ignited the spark of revolution. The pet food aisles, once brimming with promises of health and vitality, gradually transformed into corridors of doubt and uncertainty. The price tags seemed to multiply, and the assurances of quality dwindled to mere whispers in the cacophony of commercialism.

It was in the aftermath of a harrowing incident, an innocuous purchase of a seemingly harmless dog treat that nearly claimed the life of my beloved companion, that the paradigm shifted. The veil of blind trust in store-bought dog food lifted, leaving behind a quest for something more—a yearning for certainty in the nourishment bestowed upon our cherished furry friends.

SLOW COOKER DOG FOOD COOKBOOK

I embarked on a journey, one spurred by an unquenchable thirst for knowledge and a fervent determination to craft meals that not only nurtured but also delighted. Armed with my expertise and fueled by a fervor that bordered on obsession, I delved into the alchemy of homemade dog food and treats.

In the labyrinth of culinary exploration, I discovered a humble hero—my ally in the bustling orchestra of life—the slow cooker. A beacon of hope in the whirlwind of my daily routine, it became the vessel through which I sculpted culinary masterpieces for my furry companion. Its gentle embrace of ingredients transformed mere elements into symphonies of aroma and flavor, awaiting my return home—a welcoming embrace after a long day, not just for me but for my ever-grateful dog.

I vividly recall the first recipe that danced in the simmering confines of that magical slow cooker—the savory scents teasing my senses and my loyal companion's insistent tail thumping against the kitchen cabinets. The joy mirrored in those eager eyes as the first morsel touched eager lips—the unspoken approval that reverberated through the very core of my being.

Days turned into weeks, each dawn heralding a new culinary adventure. I experimented, concocted, and perfected recipes that bore the stamp of health-consciousness without compromising on the gourmet delight that every dog deserves. The joy of witnessing my four-legged friend relish each meal became the elixir that fueled my determination.

Soon, my humble kitchen became a sanctuary of innovation, and the whispers of my culinary exploits reached the ears of fellow pet owners. It began with a few friends, then acquaintances, and soon, a stream of individuals seeking respite from the maze of expensive and dubious dog foods.

One such individual, Brenda, walked into my life like a harbinger of revelation. Her eyes, once clouded with worry, now sparkled with gratitude as she extolled the virtues of homemade meals—how they had seamlessly integrated into her hectic life, saving not just money but also offering a sense of control over her beloved pet's well-being.

The seed planted by Brenda burgeoned into an epiphany. The cacophony of requests for recipes tailored to specific health concerns or dietary needs echoed the universal sentiment—a collective yearning for an alternative to the uncertainties lining the shelves of pet stores.

And so, after careful contemplation and fueled by the fervor of shared experiences and resounding praise, the idea took root—a beacon of hope in the form of a cookbook, a testament to the amalgamation of expertise, passion, and unwavering love for our furry companions.

This book, my dear reader, is not merely a compendium of recipes; it's a chronicle of dedication and a tribute to the profound connection we share with our dogs. Within these pages lie the fruits of relentless experimentation, the harvest of culinary ingenuity, and the embodiment of health-conscious nourishment crafted with love.

Come forth and traverse this journey with me. Let us embrace the art of slow-cooked dog cuisine together—a voyage of flavor, health, and unwavering devotion to our beloved companions. Welcome to a world where the scent of homemade goodness wafts through kitchens, where tails wag in eager anticipation, and where the promise of love manifests in every delectable bite.

CHAPTER 1
INTRODUCTION TO SLOW COOKER DOG FOOD

Welcome to the world of homemade dog food, where the gentle hum of the slow cooker transforms ordinary ingredients into a culinary symphony that your furry companion will adore. In this chapter, we'll embark on an exploration into the realm of slow cooker dog food, uncovering the reasons why it's a game-changer for your pet's nutrition, the myriad benefits of crafting homemade meals, and essential safety guidelines to ensure every dish you prepare is both delicious and safe for your beloved canine friend.

WHY SLOW COOKER DOG FOOD?

Imagine a cooking method that tenderly coaxes out the flavors of wholesome ingredients, retaining their nutritional value while infusing each morsel with an aroma that tantalizes your pet's senses. That's the magic of the slow cooker—a device that not only simplifies meal preparation but also elevates it to an art form.

Slow cooking isn't just about convenience; it's a technique that allows ingredients to meld together, creating a depth of flavor and texture that dogs find irresistible. The low and steady heat of the slow cooker breaks down tough fibers in meats and vegetables, ensuring that your dog receives easily digestible meals packed with nutrients.

Unlike traditional cooking methods that might denature some nutrients at higher temperatures, slow cooking retains the integrity of essential vitamins and minerals, providing your furry friend with a wholesome, nourishing meal every time.

BENEFITS OF HOMEMADE DOG FOOD

Transitioning from commercial dog food to homemade meals brings a plethora of benefits, both tangible and intangible, for your pet's overall health and well-being.

1. Quality Control: Crafting your dog's meals allows you to control the quality and source of ingredients. You can handpick fresh, high-quality produce, meats, and grains, steering clear of additives, preservatives, or questionable by-products often found in commercial dog food.

2. Tailored Nutrition: Every dog has unique nutritional requirements. Homemade meals empower you to tailor recipes to your pet's specific needs, whether they require a particular protein source, are sensitive to certain ingredients, or have health conditions that demand a specialized diet.

3. Enhanced Digestibility: Homemade dog food often leads to improved digestion. The absence of artificial additives and fillers can alleviate digestive issues, leading to better nutrient absorption and overall health.

4. Increased Palatability: The flavors of homemade meals prepared in a slow cooker are often more appealing to dogs. The slow-cooking process allows ingredients to meld, creating savory dishes that your pet will eagerly devour.

5. Healthier Skin and Coat: A balanced homemade diet can contribute to a shinier coat, healthier skin, and improved dental health, reducing the likelihood of skin issues and dental problems.

SAFETY TIPS FOR COOKING DOG FOOD

Ensuring the safety of the meals you prepare for your furry companion is paramount. Follow these essential safety guidelines to guarantee that every dish you lovingly craft is both delicious and safe for your dog:

1. Balanced Diet: Aim for a balanced diet that includes proteins, carbohydrates, fats, vitamins, and minerals. A variety of ingredients will help achieve this balance, so consider rotating recipes and ingredients.

2. Safe Handling: Practice safe food handling techniques. Wash hands thoroughly before and after handling raw ingredients to prevent cross-contamination. Keep cooking surfaces and utensils clean to avoid foodborne illnesses.

3. Avoid Harmful Ingredients: Some ingredients, such as onions, garlic, grapes, raisins, and certain spices, can be toxic to dogs. Ensure that your recipes exclude any harmful components.

4. Portion Control: Overfeeding can lead to obesity and other health issues. Follow portion guidelines based on your dog's weight and activity level to maintain a healthy weight.

5. Storage and Reheating: Store leftovers properly in airtight containers in the refrigerator or freezer. Reheat food thoroughly before serving, ensuring it's at an appropriate temperature to prevent bacterial growth.

By embracing the slow cooker as your culinary ally and adhering to these safety measures, you embark on a journey that not only nourishes your dog but also strengthens the bond you share. As we delve deeper into this cookbook, you'll discover an array of delightful recipes crafted specifically for your beloved companion, ensuring that each meal is a celebration of health, happiness, and love.

CHAPTER 2

UNDERSTANDING NUTRITIONAL NEEDS

In this chapter, we'll delve into the fundamental aspects of your dog's nutritional needs, exploring the essential nutrients vital for their health, the importance of portion control, feeding guidelines, and the art of tailoring recipes to suit various dog breeds and sizes.

NUTRIENTS ESSENTIAL FOR DOGS

Just like humans, dogs require a balanced diet that encompasses a variety of nutrients to thrive. These essential nutrients include:

1. Proteins: Vital for tissue repair, muscle growth, and overall body maintenance. Sources include meat, fish, eggs, and dairy.

2. Carbohydrates: Provide energy and aid in digestion. Opt for wholesome sources like whole grains, vegetables, and fruits.

3. Fats: Essential for healthy skin, coat, and proper functioning of organs. Incorporate healthy fats like omega-3 and omega-6 fatty acids from sources such as fish oil, flaxseed, and olive oil.

4. Vitamins: Play a crucial role in various bodily functions. Include a spectrum of vitamins, including A, B complex, C, D, and E, by incorporating a diverse range of fruits, vegetables, and supplements as needed.

5. Minerals: Necessary for strong bones, teeth, and overall well-being. Calcium, phosphorus, potassium, magnesium, and others can be obtained from meats, vegetables, and supplements.

6. Water: Essential for hydration and the functioning of every cell in the body. Ensure your dog has constant access to fresh, clean water.

Balancing these nutrients in your dog's diet is essential for their overall health, ensuring they receive a well-rounded and complete nutritional profile.

PORTION CONTROL AND FEEDING GUIDELINES

Understanding portion control and feeding guidelines is crucial to maintaining your dog's health and preventing issues like obesity or malnutrition.

1. Weight and Activity Level: Consider your dog's weight, age, and activity level when determining portion sizes. Active dogs may require more calories, while older or less active dogs may need fewer calories to maintain a healthy weight.

2. Follow Recommended Portions: Consult your veterinarian or use feeding guidelines provided on commercial dog food packages as a baseline for portion control. Adjust as needed based on your dog's individual needs.

3. Scheduled Meals: Establish a consistent feeding schedule, offering meals at specific times each day. Avoid free-feeding to better monitor your dog's food intake.

4. Monitor Body Condition: Keep an eye on your dog's body condition score. Ideally, you want to maintain a healthy weight. Adjust portion sizes accordingly if your dog is gaining or losing weight.

5. Avoid Overfeeding: Overfeeding can lead to obesity, which predisposes dogs to various health issues. Be mindful of treats and table scraps, as they contribute to overall calorie intake.

TAILORING RECIPES FOR DIFFERENT DOG BREEDS AND SIZES

Dogs come in various shapes, sizes, and breeds, each with its unique nutritional needs. Tailoring recipes to suit these differences ensures that every dog receives a diet optimized for their well-being.

1. Small Breeds: Small dogs often have higher metabolic rates and smaller stomachs. Consider nutrient-dense recipes with smaller kibble sizes or softer textures for easier digestion.

2. Large Breeds: Large breeds may be more prone to joint issues. Include ingredients like glucosamine and chondroitin for joint health, and opt for diets rich in high-quality protein for muscle maintenance.

3. Specific Breeds: Certain breeds may have breed-specific health concerns. Research and consult with your veterinarian to address these concerns through diet. For example, breeds prone to urinary issues might benefit from recipes with controlled mineral content.

4. Puppies and Seniors: Puppies require diets rich in protein and fats to support growth, while senior dogs may need fewer calories and certain supplements to aid aging joints and digestion.

By understanding your dog's nutritional requirements and tailoring their meals accordingly, you pave the way for a healthy, vibrant life for your furry friend.

CHAPTER 3
SLOW COOKING BASICS FOR DOG FOOD

In this chapter, we'll unravel the art and science of using a slow cooker to craft delectable and nutritious meals for your furry companion. Understanding the nuances of choosing the right ingredients, mastering the safe usage of a slow cooker, and navigating cooking times and temperatures will empower you to create sumptuous slow cooker dog food recipes with ease.

CHOOSING THE RIGHT INGREDIENTS

The cornerstone of crafting nutritious and palatable slow cooker dog food lies in the ingredients you select. Here are some tips to ensure you choose wisely:

1. High-Quality Proteins: Opt for lean meats like chicken, turkey, beef, or fish as primary protein sources. Avoid processed meats and those high in fat or additives.

2. Healthy Carbohydrates: Incorporate whole grains like brown rice, quinoa, or barley for energy. Vegetables like sweet potatoes, carrots, peas, and green beans are excellent sources of fiber and vitamins.

3. Beneficial Fats: Include healthy fats from sources like fish oil, olive oil, or coconut oil to promote a shiny coat and overall well-being.

4. Avoid Harmful Ingredients: Some foods, such as onions, garlic, chocolate, grapes, and certain spices, are toxic to dogs. Ensure your ingredient list excludes these harmful components.

5. Supplements: Consider adding supplements like calcium, glucosamine, or probiotics as recommended by your veterinarian to address specific health concerns.

TIPS FOR USING A SLOW COOKER SAFELY

Mastering the art of using a slow cooker safely is essential to ensure that every meal you prepare is not just delicious but also free from any potential hazards. Here's how you can do it:

1. Prep and Handling: Wash your hands, utensils, and cooking surfaces thoroughly before and after handling raw ingredients to prevent cross-contamination.

2. Thaw Ingredients: Ensure all meats and other perishables are fully thawed before adding them to the slow cooker to avoid uneven cooking and bacterial growth.

3. Layer Ingredients Wisely: Place denser and tougher ingredients, such as meats and root vegetables, at the bottom of the slow cooker to ensure even cooking.

4. Monitor Temperatures: Ensure the slow cooker reaches and maintains a safe cooking temperature. Use a food thermometer to confirm that meats reach an internal temperature of at least 165°F (74°C) to eliminate harmful bacteria.

5. Avoid Overfilling: Fill the slow cooker to the recommended level to prevent spillage or uneven cooking. Overfilling may lead to insufficient cooking or potential food safety issues.

6. Slow Cooking Overnight: While it's tempting to leave the slow cooker running overnight, it's safer to prepare meals during waking hours to monitor the cooking process.

COOKING TIMES AND TEMPERATURES

Understanding the cooking times and temperatures for slow cooker dog food recipes is key to achieving perfectly cooked meals bursting with flavor and nutrients:

1. Low and Slow: The beauty of a slow cooker lies in its low and consistent cooking temperatures. Most dog food recipes benefit from cooking on low heat settings for 6-8 hours to tenderize ingredients and develop flavors.

2. Adjust for Ingredients: Tougher cuts of meat or larger chunks may require longer cooking times, while softer vegetables or grains might need shorter durations. Adapt recipes accordingly.

3. Careful Timing: Avoid opening the slow cooker unnecessarily during the cooking process, as this releases heat and prolongs the cooking time.

4. Test for Doneness: Use a fork to check the tenderness of meats and vegetables. They should be easily pierced but not overly mushy.

Mastering the fundamentals of selecting ingredients, safe usage of a slow cooker, and understanding cooking times and temperatures lays the groundwork for crafting delectable slow cooker dog food recipes

CHAPTER 4
MEAT-BASED RECIPES

BEEF-BASED MEALS

1) Beef and Sweet Potato Stew

Cook Time: 6 hours on low

Servings: 4-6

Ingredients:

- 1 pound lean beef, diced
- 2 sweet potatoes, peeled and chopped
- 1 cup green beans, trimmed and chopped
- 1 cup carrots, sliced
- 4 cups beef broth
- 1 tablespoon olive oil

Instructions:

1) In a skillet, heat olive oil over medium-high heat. Brown the diced beef for 3-4 minutes.
2) Place the browned beef, sweet potatoes, green beans, and carrots into the slow cooker.
3) Pour beef broth over the ingredients.
4) Cook on low for 6 hours.

5) Allow it to cool before serving.

Nutritional Information:

Calories: 250 | Protein: 22g | Fat: 8g | Carbohydrates: 20g

Tips:

- Remove excess fat from the beef before cooking to reduce the stew's fat content.
- Ensure vegetables are chopped into appropriate sizes for your dog's consumption.

2) Beef and Carrot Casserole

Cook Time: 4-5 hours on low

Servings: 3-4

Ingredients:

- 1.5 pounds beef stew meat, cubed
- 1 cup carrots, sliced
- 1 cup peas
- 1 cup brown rice
- 3 cups beef broth

Instructions:

1) Layer beef stew meat, carrots, peas, and brown rice in the slow cooker.
2) Pour beef broth over the ingredients.
3) Cook on low for 4-5 hours until the meat is tender.
4) Allow it to cool before serving.

Nutritional Information:

Calories: 320 | Protein: 28g | Fat: 10g | Carbohydrates: 25g

Tips:

- Opt for lean cuts of beef to reduce the fat content.
- Use low-sodium beef broth or homemade broth to control sodium levels.

3) Beef and Spinach Stew

Cook Time: 5-6 hours on low

Servings: 4-5

Ingredients:

- 1.5 pounds beef chuck, cut into chunks
- 2 cups spinach, chopped
- 1 cup peas
- 1 cup chopped tomatoes
- 2 cups beef stock

Instructions:

1) Place beef chunks, spinach, peas, and chopped tomatoes in the slow cooker.
2) Pour beef stock over the ingredients.
3) Cook on low for 5-6 hours until the beef is tender.
4) Allow it to cool before serving.

Nutritional Information:

Calories: 290 | Protein: 26g | Fat: 12g | Carbohydrates: 18g

Tips:

- Use fresh, quality ingredients for the best flavor.
- Adjust seasoning to your dog's taste preferences, avoiding added salt.

4) Beef and Quinoa Medley

Cook Time: 4 hours on low

Servings: 3-4

Ingredients:

- 1 pound beef stew meat, cubed
- 1 cup quinoa, rinsed
- 1 cup carrots, diced
- 1 cup green peas
- 3 cups low-sodium beef broth

Instructions:

1) Layer beef stew meat, quinoa, carrots, and green peas in the slow cooker.
2) Pour beef broth over the ingredients.
3) Cook on low for 4 hours or until the beef is cooked through.
4) Allow it to cool before serving.

Nutritional Information:

Calories: 290 | Protein: 24g | Fat: 8g | Carbohydrates: 30g

Tips:

- Rinse quinoa thoroughly before using to remove its natural coating, which can taste bitter to some dogs.
- Adjust the cooking time if needed, as quinoa might cook faster than other ingredients.

5) Beef and Pumpkin Stew

Cook Time: 5-6 hours on low

Servings: 4-5

Ingredients:

- 1.5 pounds beef chuck, cut into cubes
- 1 cup canned pumpkin puree
- 1 cup broccoli florets, chopped
- 1 cup barley
- 2 cups beef broth

Instructions:

1) Combine beef cubes, pumpkin puree, broccoli, barley, and beef broth in the slow cooker.
2) Stir to mix the ingredients well.
3) Cook on low for 5-6 hours until the beef is tender.
4) Allow it to cool before serving.

Nutritional Information:

Calories: 310 | Protein: 26g | Fat: 10g | Carbohydrates: 25g

Tips:

- Choose plain, unsweetened pumpkin puree without added spices or sugars.
- Barley adds fiber; however, if your dog has a sensitive stomach, consider using a smaller quantity.

CHICKEN-BASED MEALS

6) Chicken and Brown Rice Delight

Cook Time: 4 hours on low

Servings: 4-6

Ingredients:

- 1 pound boneless, skinless chicken breasts, cubed
- 1 cup brown rice
- 1 cup sweet potatoes, diced
- 1 cup peas
- 3 cups chicken broth

Instructions:

1) Combine chicken cubes, brown rice, sweet potatoes, peas, and chicken broth in the slow cooker.
2) Stir to mix the ingredients well.
3) Cook on low for 4 hours or until the chicken is cooked through.
4) Allow it to cool before serving.

Nutritional Information:

Calories: 280 | Protein: 26g | Fat: 4g | Carbohydrates: 35g

Tips:

- Use brown rice for added fiber and nutrients compared to white rice.
- Adjust the amount of broth to achieve the desired consistency for your dog's preference.

7) Chicken and Vegetable Mix

Cook Time: 3-4 hours on low

Servings: 3-4

Ingredients:

- 1.5 pounds boneless, skinless chicken thighs, chopped
- 2 cups carrots, sliced
- 1 cup green beans, chopped
- 1 cup potatoes, diced
- 2 cups chicken stock

Instructions:

1) Place chicken thighs, carrots, green beans, potatoes, and chicken stock in the slow cooker.
2) Mix the ingredients thoroughly.
3) Cook on low for 3-4 hours until the chicken is tender.
4) Allow it to cool before serving.

Nutritional Information:

Calories: 320 | Protein: 30g | Fat: 6g | Carbohydrates: 30g

Tips:

- Use chicken thighs for a richer flavor, but trim excess fat to make it healthier.
- Monitor the size of vegetable chunks, ensuring they're suitable for your dog's consumption.

8) Chicken and Pumpkin Stew

Cook Time: 5-6 hours on low

Servings: 4-5

Ingredients:

- 1.5 pounds boneless, skinless chicken breasts, cut into cubes
- 1 cup pumpkin puree
- 1 cup spinach, chopped
- 1 cup quinoa
- 3 cups low-sodium chicken broth

Instructions:

1) Combine chicken cubes, pumpkin puree, spinach, quinoa, and chicken broth in the slow cooker.
2) Stir the mixture well.
3) Cook on low for 5-6 hours until the chicken is thoroughly cooked.
4) Allow it to cool before serving.

Nutritional Information:

Calories: 310 | Protein: 28g | Fat: 5g | Carbohydrates: 30g

Tips:

- Opt for fresh, plain pumpkin puree without added spices or sugars.
- Rinse quinoa thoroughly before use to remove any bitterness.

9) Chicken and Potato Medley

Cook Time: 4-5 hours on low

- **Servings:** 4-6

Ingredients:

- 1 pound boneless, skinless chicken thighs, cut into cubes
- 2 cups potatoes, diced
- 1 cup carrots, sliced
- 1 cup green peas
- 3 cups low-sodium chicken broth

Instructions:

1) Combine chicken thigh cubes, potatoes, carrots, green peas, and chicken broth in the slow cooker.
2) Stir well to ensure even distribution of ingredients.
3) Cook on low for 4-5 hours until the chicken is thoroughly cooked.
4) Allow it to cool before serving.

Nutritional Information:

Calories: 290 | Protein: 26g | Fat: 4g | Carbohydrates: 30g

Tips:

- Use skinless chicken to reduce fat content in the dish.
- Feel free to substitute sweet potatoes for regular ones for added nutrients.

10)   Chicken and Broccoli Delight

Cook Time: 3-4 hours on low

Servings: 3-4

Ingredients:

- 1.5 pounds boneless, skinless chicken breasts, chopped
- 2 cups broccoli florets
- 1 cup cauliflower florets
- 1 cup brown rice
- 3 cups chicken stock

Instructions:

1) Layer chicken breast pieces, broccoli, cauliflower, brown rice, and chicken stock in the slow cooker.
2) Mix the ingredients thoroughly.
3) Cook on low for 3-4 hours until the chicken is tender.
4) Allow it to cool before serving.

Nutritional Information:

Calories: 310 | Protein: 28g | Fat: 5g | Carbohydrates: 35g

Tips:

- Opt for fresh broccoli and cauliflower for maximum nutrient retention.
- Check the brown rice halfway through the cooking process to ensure it's fully cooked.

TURKEY-BASED MEALS

11) Turkey and Pumpkin Medley

Cook Time: 4-5 hours on low

Servings: 4-6

Ingredients:

- 1 pound ground turkey
- 1 cup pumpkin puree
- 1 cup carrots, sliced
- 1 cup green beans, chopped
- 3 cups low-sodium turkey or chicken broth

Instructions:

1) Brown the ground turkey in a skillet until fully cooked, then drain excess fat.
2) Transfer the cooked turkey, pumpkin puree, carrots, green beans, and broth to the slow cooker.
3) Mix the ingredients thoroughly.
4) Cook on low for 4-5 hours.
5) Allow it to cool before serving.

Nutritional Information:

Calories: 240 | Protein: 20g | Fat: 8g | Carbohydrates: 20g

Tips:

- Use plain pumpkin puree without added sugars or spices.
- Adjust the consistency by adding more or less broth based on your dog's preference.

12)   Turkey and Quinoa Surprise

Cook Time: 3-4 hours on low

Servings: 3-4

Ingredients:

- 1 pound ground turkey
- 1 cup quinoa, rinsed
- 1 cup sweet potatoes, diced
- 1 cup peas
- 2 cups low-sodium turkey or chicken broth

Instructions:

1) Brown the ground turkey in a skillet until fully cooked, then drain excess fat.
2) In the slow cooker, combine the cooked turkey, quinoa, sweet potatoes, peas, and broth. Mix well.
3) Cook on low for 3-4 hours.
4) Allow it to cool before serving.

Nutritional Information:

Calories: 280 | Protein: 22g | Fat: 9g | Carbohydrates: 25g

Tips:

- Rinse quinoa thoroughly to remove its bitter coating.
- Adjust the vegetable quantities based on your dog's preferences.

13) Turkey and Spinach Stew

Cook Time: 5-6 hours on low

Servings: 4-5

Ingredients:

- 1.5 pounds ground turkey
- 2 cups spinach, chopped
- 1 cup carrots, sliced
- 1 cup brown rice
- 3 cups low-sodium turkey or chicken broth

Instructions:

1) Brown the ground turkey in a skillet until fully cooked, then drain excess fat.
2) Place the cooked turkey, spinach, carrots, brown rice, and broth into the slow cooker. Mix well.
3) Cook on low for 5-6 hours.
4) Allow it to cool before serving.

Nutritional Information:

Calories: 310 | Protein: 25g | Fat: 10g | Carbohydrates: 30g

Tips:

- Use lean ground turkey for a healthier option.
- Adjust the cooking time if needed, ensuring the rice is fully cooked.

14)   Turkey and Lentil Stew

Cook Time: 4-5 hours on low

Servings: 3-4

Ingredients:

- 1 pound ground turkey
- 1 cup lentils, rinsed
- 1 cup bell peppers, diced
- 1 cup zucchini, sliced
- 2 cups low-sodium turkey or chicken broth

Instructions:

1) Brown the ground turkey in a skillet until fully cooked, then drain excess fat.
2) Combine the cooked turkey, rinsed lentils, bell peppers, zucchini, and broth in the slow cooker. Mix the ingredients thoroughly.
3) Cook on low for 4-5 hours.
4) Allow it to cool before serving.

Nutritional Information:

Calories: 290 | Protein: 24g | Fat: 8g | Carbohydrates: 25g

Tips:

- Rinse the lentils thoroughly to remove any debris or residue.
- Adjust the quantity of broth to achieve the desired consistency.

15) Turkey and Sweet Potato Casserole

Cook Time: 5-6 hours on low

Servings: 4-5

Ingredients:

- 1.5 pounds ground turkey
- 2 cups sweet potatoes, diced
- 1 cup green peas
- 1 cup carrots, sliced
- 3 cups low-sodium turkey or chicken broth

Instructions:

1) Brown the ground turkey in a skillet until fully cooked, then drain excess fat.
2) In the slow cooker, combine the cooked turkey, sweet potatoes, green peas, carrots, and broth. Mix the ingredients thoroughly.
3) Cook on low for 5-6 hours.
4) Allow it to cool before serving.

Nutritional Information:

Calories: 300 | Protein: 26g | Fat: 9g | Carbohydrates: 30g

Tips:

- Peel sweet potatoes before dicing them for easier digestion.
- Adjust the vegetable quantities according to your dog's preferences.

FISH-BASED MEALS

16)   Salmon and Sweet Potato Blend

Cook Time: 3-4 hours on low

Servings: 3-4

Ingredients:

- 1 pound salmon fillets, deboned and cut into chunks
- 2 sweet potatoes, peeled and diced
- 1 cup green beans, trimmed and chopped
- 3 cups fish or vegetable broth

Instructions:

1) Place salmon chunks, sweet potatoes, green beans, and broth into the slow cooker.
2) Mix the ingredients thoroughly.
3) Cook on low for 3-4 hours until the salmon is cooked and sweet potatoes are tender.
4) Allow it to cool before serving.

Nutritional Information:

Calories: 280 | Protein: 25g | Fat: 10g | Carbohydrates: 20g

Tips:

- Remove salmon skin before cooking for easier digestion.
- Ensure fish bones are completely removed before serving to your dog.

17) Tuna and Green Pea Delight

Cook Time: 2-3 hours on low

Servings: 2-3

Ingredients:

- 1 can tuna in water (drained)
- 1 cup green peas
- 1 cup carrots, sliced
- 2 cups fish or vegetable broth

Instructions:

1) In the slow cooker, combine drained tuna, green peas, carrots, and broth.
2) Mix well.
3) Cook on low for 2-3 hours.
4) Allow it to cool before serving.

Nutritional Information:

Calories: 200 | Protein: 18g | Fat: 5g | Carbohydrates: 15g

Tips:

- Use tuna packed in water without added salt or seasoning.
- Check for any bones in canned tuna before adding it to the slow cooker.

18) Cod and Potato Casserole

Cook Time: 4-5 hours on low

Servings: 4-5

Ingredients:

- 1 pound cod fillets, cut into chunks
- 2 cups potatoes, diced
- 1 cup carrots, sliced
- 1 cup celery, chopped
- 3 cups fish or vegetable broth

Instructions:

1) Layer cod chunks, potatoes, carrots, celery, and broth in the slow cooker.
2) Mix the ingredients thoroughly.
3) Cook on low for 4-5 hours until the fish is cooked through.
4) Allow it to cool before serving.

Nutritional Information:

Calories: 240 | Protein: 20g | Fat: 2g | Carbohydrates: 25g

Tips:

- Use fresh cod fillets and ensure they are boneless.
- Adjust the size of the potato chunks for your dog's preference.

19) Tilapia and Vegetable Medley

Cook Time: 3-4 hours on low

Servings: 3-4

Ingredients:

- 1 pound tilapia fillets, cut into chunks
- 1 cup bell peppers, diced
- 1 cup broccoli florets
- 1 cup cauliflower florets
- 3 cups fish or vegetable broth

Instructions:

1) Combine tilapia chunks, bell peppers, broccoli, cauliflower, and broth in the slow cooker.
2) Mix the ingredients thoroughly.
3) Cook on low for 3-4 hours until the fish is fully cooked.
4) Allow it to cool before serving.

Nutritional Information:

Calories: 220 | Protein: 25g | Fat: 3g | Carbohydrates: 20g

Tips:

- Opt for fresh vegetables to retain maximum nutrients.
- Check the tilapia for any remaining bones or skin before adding it to the slow cooker.

20)   Sardine and Carrot Stew

Cook Time: 2-3 hours on low

Servings: 2-3

Ingredients:

- 1 can sardines in water (drained)
- 1 cup carrots, sliced
- 1 cup peas
- 2 cups fish or vegetable broth

Instructions:

1) In the slow cooker, combine drained sardines, carrots, peas, and broth.
2) Mix well.
3) Cook on low for 2-3 hours.
4) Allow it to cool before serving.

Nutritional Information:

Calories: 180 | Protein: 15g | Fat: 8g | Carbohydrates: 15g

Tips:

- Use sardines packed in water without added salt or seasoning.
- Drain and rinse canned sardines to reduce sodium content before adding to the slow cooker.

NOTE FROM THE AUTHOR!

Hello there, before we dive into the next chapter, i want to extend my heartfelt gratitude to you for joining me on this remarkable journey. Exploring the realm of homemade dog food and nutrition can spark curiosity and raise questions. As a fellow dog lover, I'm here to be your guiding light.

Your decision to invest in this book means everything to me. I'm dedicated to supporting you at every turn. Whether you seek clarity, guidance, or a deeper understanding, don't hesitate to reach out via email at: **drdorismeanyvet@gmail.com**

I promise to personally respond within 24 hours, eager to assist as you strive for improved wellness. Your feedback and questions are immensely valuable. I genuinely appreciate the privilege of accompanying you through this process.

CHAPTER 5
SPECIALIZED DIETS AND HEALTH CONSIDERATIONS

RECIPES FOR SENIOR DOGS

21)   Chicken and Brown Rice Stew for Senior Dogs

Cook Time: 4-5 hours on low

Servings: 3-4

Ingredients:

- 1 pound boneless, skinless chicken thighs, chopped
- 1 cup brown rice
- 1 cup carrots, sliced
- 1 cup green beans, chopped
- 3 cups low-sodium chicken broth

Instructions:

1) Combine chicken thighs, brown rice, carrots, green beans, and chicken broth in the slow cooker.
2) Mix the ingredients thoroughly.
3) Cook on low for 4-5 hours until the chicken is tender and rice is cooked.
4) Allow it to cool before serving.

Nutritional Information:

Calories: 290 | Protein: 25g | Fat: 8g | Carbohydrates: 25g

Tips:

- Use boneless chicken to make it easier for senior dogs to chew.
- Soak the brown rice for a few hours before cooking to aid digestion.

22) Turkey and Pumpkin Mash for Senior Dogs

Cook Time: 3-4 hours on low

Servings: 2-3

Ingredients:

- 1 pound ground turkey
- 1 cup pumpkin puree
- 1 cup peas
- 1 cup sweet potatoes, diced
- 2 cups low-sodium turkey or vegetable broth

Instructions:

1) Brown the ground turkey in a skillet until fully cooked, then drain excess fat.
2) In the slow cooker, mix the cooked turkey, pumpkin puree, peas, sweet potatoes, and broth.
3) Cook on low for 3-4 hours until the sweet potatoes are tender.
4) Allow it to cool before serving.

Nutritional Information:

Calories: 260 | Protein: 22g | Fat: 8g | Carbohydrates: 20g

Tips:

- Use lean ground turkey for a healthier option.
- Mash or blend the mixture for dogs with dental issues or difficulty chewing.

23) Beef and Barley Stew for Senior Dogs

Cook Time: 4-5 hours on low

Servings: 3-4

Ingredients:

- 1 pound beef stew meat, cubed
- 1 cup barley
- 1 cup carrots, sliced
- 1 cup spinach, chopped
- 3 cups low-sodium beef broth

Instructions:

1) Layer beef stew meat, barley, carrots, spinach, and beef broth in the slow cooker.
2) Mix well.
3) Cook on low for 4-5 hours until the beef is tender.
4) Allow it to cool before serving.

Nutritional Information:

Calories: 300 | Protein: 26g | Fat: 10g | Carbohydrates: 25g

Tips:

- Cut the beef into smaller pieces for easier consumption by senior dogs.
- Adjust the amount of liquid for desired consistency.

24) Salmon and Sweet Potato Stew for Senior Dogs

Cook Time: 3-4 hours on low

Servings: 2-3

Ingredients:

- 1 pound salmon fillets, deboned and cut into chunks
- 2 sweet potatoes, peeled and diced
- 1 cup green peas
- 2 cups fish or vegetable broth

Instructions:

1) Place salmon chunks, sweet potatoes, green peas, and broth into the slow cooker.
2) Mix the ingredients thoroughly.
3) Cook on low for 3-4 hours until the salmon is cooked through and sweet potatoes are tender.
4) Allow it to cool before serving.

Nutritional Information:

Calories: 280 | Protein: 25g | Fat: 10g | Carbohydrates: 20g

Tips:

- Remove salmon skin before cooking for easier digestion.
- Adjust the cooking time to prevent overcooking the fish.

25) Turkey and Vegetable Medley for Senior Dogs

Cook Time: 4-5 hours on low

Servings: 3-4

Ingredients:

- 1 pound ground turkey
- 1 cup carrots, sliced
- 1 cup green beans, chopped
- 1 cup potatoes, diced
- 3 cups low-sodium turkey or vegetable broth

Instructions:

1) Brown the ground turkey in a skillet until fully cooked, then drain excess fat.
2) Combine cooked turkey, carrots, green beans, potatoes, and broth in the slow cooker. Mix well.
3) Cook on low for 4-5 hours until vegetables are tender.
4) Allow it to cool before serving.

Nutritional Information:

Calories: 260 | Protein: 22g | Fat: 8g | Carbohydrates: 20g

Tips:

- Use lean ground turkey to reduce fat content.
- Adjust the size of vegetable pieces for senior dogs with dental issues.

VEGETARIAN OPTIONS

26)   Sweet Potato and Lentil Stew

Cook Time: 4 hours on high or 6-8 hours on low

Servings: 4-6

Ingredients:

- 2 cups sweet potatoes, diced
- 1 cup lentils
- 4 cups vegetable broth
- 1 cup carrots, chopped
- 1 cup green beans, chopped

Instructions:

1) Combine all ingredients in the slow cooker.
2) Cook on high for 4 hours or on low for 6-8 hours until lentils are tender.
3) Mash or blend for a smoother texture.

Nutritional Information:

Per serving - Calories: 180, Protein: 8g, Fat: 0.5g, Carbohydrates: 35g, Fiber: 9g

Tips:

- Add a sprinkle of turmeric for its anti-inflammatory properties.
- Ensure lentils are well-cooked before serving to aid digestion.

27)   Quinoa and Vegetable Medley

Cook Time: 2-3 hours on high or 4-6 hours on low

Servings: 4-6

Ingredients:

- 1 cup quinoa, rinsed
- 2 cups mixed vegetables (broccoli, cauliflower, peas)
- 3 cups vegetable broth

Instructions:

1) Place all ingredients in the slow cooker.
2) Cook on high for 2-3 hours or on low for 4-6 hours until quinoa is cooked and vegetables are tender.

Nutritional Information:

Per serving - Calories: 220, Protein: 8g, Fat: 3g, Carbohydrates: 40g, Fiber: 8g

Tips:

- Use low sodium broth to control sodium intake.
- Mix in a tablespoon of coconut oil after cooking for added healthy fats.

28) Pumpkin and Brown Rice Delight

Cook Time: 3-4 hours on high or 6-8 hours on low

Servings: 4-6

Ingredients:

- 2 cups pumpkin puree
- 1 cup brown rice, uncooked
- 4 cups water or vegetable broth

Instructions:

1) Combine pumpkin, brown rice, and liquid in the slow cooker.
2) Cook on high for 3-4 hours or on low for 6-8 hours until rice is tender.

Nutritional Information:

Per serving - Calories: 160, Protein: 3g, Fat: 1g, Carbohydrates: 35g, Fiber: 5g

Tips:

- Opt for fresh pumpkin puree or canned puree without added sugars.
- Brown rice adds fiber and nutrients.

29)   Spinach and Chickpea Stew

Cook Time: 4-5 hours on high or 6-8 hours on low

Servings: 4-6

Ingredients:

- 2 cups chickpeas, cooked
- 2 cups spinach, chopped
- 1 cup diced tomatoes
- 4 cups vegetable broth
- 1 teaspoon turmeric

Instructions:

1) Combine all ingredients in the slow cooker.
2) Cook on high for 4-5 hours or on low for 6-8 hours until flavors meld.

Nutritional Information:

Per serving - Calories: 200, Protein: 10g, Fat: 3g, Carbohydrates: 35g, Fiber: 9g

Tips:

- Mash or blend ingredients for easier digestion.
- Chickpeas offer a protein boost.

30) Zucchini and Potato Casserole

Cook Time: 3-4 hours on high or 6-8 hours on low

Servings: 4-6

Ingredients:

- 2 cups zucchini, sliced
- 2 cups potatoes, diced
- 1 cup green peas
- 3 cups vegetable broth
- 1 teaspoon dried parsley

Instructions:

1) Layer zucchini, potatoes, and peas in the slow cooker.
2) Pour vegetable broth over the vegetables, sprinkle with parsley.
3) Cook on high for 3-4 hours or on low for 6-8 hours until potatoes are tender.

Nutritional Information:

Per serving - Calories: 180, Protein: 5g, Fat: 1g, Carbohydrates: 40g, Fiber: 7g

Tips:

- Add a pinch of powdered kelp for additional minerals.
- Ensure the potatoes are cooked thoroughly before serving.

31) **Butternut Squash and Barley Stew**

Cook Time: 4-5 hours on high or 6-8 hours on low

Servings: 4-6

Ingredients:

- 2 cups butternut squash, cubed
- 1 cup barley, rinsed
- 4 cups low-sodium vegetable broth
- 1 cup green beans, chopped

Instructions:

1) Combine butternut squash, barley, and vegetable broth in the slow cooker.
2) Cook on high for 4-5 hours or on low for 6-8 hours until squash and barley are tender.
3) Add green beans during the last hour of cooking.

Nutritional Information:

Per serving - Calories: 190, Protein: 5g, Fat: 1g, Carbohydrates: 40g, Fiber: 9g

Tips:

- Soak barley overnight for improved digestibility.
- Avoid adding salt or seasonings containing onion or garlic.

RECIPES FOR DOGS WITH ALLERGIES OR SENSITIVITIES

32)   Lamb and Potato Stew (Limited Ingredients)

Cook Time: 4-5 hours on low

Servings: 3-4

Ingredients:

- 1 pound boneless lamb, cubed
- 2 sweet potatoes, peeled and diced
- 1 cup green beans, chopped
- 3 cups low-sodium lamb or vegetable broth

Instructions:

1) Combine cubed lamb, sweet potatoes, green beans, and broth in the slow cooker.
2) Mix thoroughly.
3) Cook on low for 4-5 hours until lamb is tender and sweet potatoes are cooked.
4) Allow it to cool before serving.

Nutritional Information:

Calories: 320 | Protein: 25g | Fat: 12g | Carbohydrates: 30g

Tips:

- Use boneless lamb to reduce fat content.
- Trim excess fat from the lamb before cooking for sensitive stomachs.

33)   Turkey and Rice Congee (Gentle on Digestion)

Cook Time: 3-4 hours on low

Servings: 3-4

Ingredients:

- 1 pound ground turkey
- 1 cup white rice, rinsed
- 4 cups low-sodium chicken or turkey broth

Instructions:

1) Brown the ground turkey in a skillet until fully cooked, then drain excess fat.
2) In the slow cooker, combine cooked turkey, rinsed white rice, and broth.
3) Mix well.
4) Cook on low for 3-4 hours until rice is soft and the mixture thickens.
5) Allow it to cool before serving.

Nutritional Information:

Calories: 280 | Protein: 20g | Fat: 8g | Carbohydrates: 30g

Tips:

- Use white rice, as it's easily digestible.
- Add a little more broth if the congee becomes too thick during cooking.

34)   Salmon and Carrot Casserole (Omega-3 Rich)

Cook Time: 3-4 hours on low

Servings: 2-3

Ingredients:

- 1 pound salmon fillets, deboned and cubed
- 2 cups carrots, sliced
- 1 cup peas
- 2 cups fish or vegetable broth

Instructions:

1) Place salmon, carrots, peas, and broth into the slow cooker.
2) Mix gently.
3) Cook on low for 3-4 hours until salmon is cooked and carrots are tender.
4) Allow it to cool before serving.

Nutritional Information:

Calories: 260 | Protein: 25g | Fat: 12g | Carbohydrates: 20g

Tips:

- Remove salmon skin for easier digestion.
- Use fresh or frozen salmon without added seasonings.

35)   Beef and Parsnip Stew (Alternative Protein Source)

Cook Time: 4-5 hours on low

Servings: 3-4

Ingredients:

- 1 pound beef stew meat, cubed
- 2 parsnips, peeled and sliced
- 1 cup green peas
- 3 cups low-sodium beef or vegetable broth

Instructions:

1) Layer beef stew meat, parsnips, green peas, and broth in the slow cooker.
2) Mix gently.
3) Cook on low for 4-5 hours until beef is tender.
4) Allow it to cool before serving.

Nutritional Information:

Calories: 320 | Protein: 25g | Fat: 12g | Carbohydrates: 30g

Tips:

- Opt for lean cuts of beef to minimize fat.
- Monitor portion sizes based on your dog's dietary needs.

WEIGHT MANAGEMENT RECIPES

36) Pork and Apple Casserole

Cook Time: 4-5 hours on low

Servings: 3-4

Ingredients:

- 1 pound pork loin, cubed
- 2 apples, cored and sliced
- 1 cup sweet potatoes, diced
- 2 cups low-sodium vegetable or pork broth

Instructions:

1) Combine pork loin, apples, sweet potatoes, and broth in the slow cooker.
2) Mix gently.
3) Cook on low for 4-5 hours until pork is cooked through and apples are soft.
4) Allow it to cool before serving.

Nutritional Information:

Calories: 240 | Protein: 25g | Fat: 8g | Carbohydrates: 20g

Tips:

- Use lean pork cuts and trim excess fat.
- Apples offer natural sweetness without added sugars.

37) Lamb and Barley Stew

Cook Time: 4-5 hours on low

Servings: 3-4

Ingredients:

- 1 pound lamb stew meat, cubed
- 1 cup barley
- 1 cup carrots, sliced
- 3 cups low-sodium lamb or vegetable broth

Instructions:

1) Layer lamb stew meat, barley, carrots, and broth in the slow cooker.
2) Mix gently.
3) Cook on low for 4-5 hours until lamb is tender and barley is cooked.
4) Allow it to cool before serving.

Nutritional Information:

Calories: 280 | Protein: 22g | Fat: 10g | Carbohydrates: 25g

Tips:

- Trim visible fat from lamb to reduce calorie content.
- Barley provides a good source of fiber.

38)   Duck and Pumpkin Stew

Cook Time: 3-4 hours on low

Servings: 2-3

Ingredients:

- 1 pound duck breast, diced
- 1 cup pumpkin puree
- 1 cup green peas
- 2 cups low-sodium vegetable or duck broth

Instructions:

1) Combine duck breast, pumpkin puree, green peas, and broth in the slow cooker.
2) Mix thoroughly.
3) Cook on low for 3-4 hours until duck is cooked and flavors meld.
4) Allow it to cool before serving.

Nutritional Information:

Calories: 260 | Protein: 24g | Fat: 12g | Carbohydrates: 15g

Tips:

- Duck breast offers a lean protein source.
- Pumpkin is gentle on digestion and provides essential nutrients.

39)   Venison and Cranberry Stew

Cook Time: 4-5 hours on low

Servings: 3-4

Ingredients:

- 1 pound venison stew meat, cubed
- 1 cup cranberries (unsweetened), fresh or frozen
- 1 cup potatoes, diced
- 3 cups low-sodium vegetable or beef broth

Instructions:

1) Combine venison stew meat, cranberries, potatoes, and broth in the slow cooker.
2) Mix gently.
3) Cook on low for 4-5 hours until venison is tender.
4) Allow it to cool before serving.

Nutritional Information:

Calories: 300 | Protein: 25g | Fat: 10g | Carbohydrates: 25g

Tips:

- Trim visible fat from venison for a leaner option.
- Cranberries add a touch of tartness and antioxidants.

HEALTH-BOOSTING RECIPES

40)   Turkey and Blueberry Stew

Cook Time: 4-5 hours on low

Servings: 3-4

Ingredients:

- 1 pound ground turkey
- 1 cup blueberries (fresh or frozen)
- 1 cup sweet potatoes, diced
- 3 cups low-sodium turkey or vegetable broth

Instructions:

1) Brown the ground turkey in a skillet until fully cooked, then drain excess fat.
2) Combine cooked turkey, blueberries, sweet potatoes, and broth in the slow cooker.
3) Mix well.
4) Cook on low for 4-5 hours until sweet potatoes are tender.
5) Allow it to cool before serving.

Nutritional Information:

Calories: 260 | Protein: 22g | Fat: 8g | Carbohydrates: 25g

Tips:

- Blueberries are rich in antioxidants and offer various health benefits.
- Choose lean ground turkey for lower fat content.

41)   Salmon and Kale Delight

Cook Time: 3-4 hours on low

Servings: 2-3

Ingredients:

- 1 pound salmon fillets, deboned and cut into chunks
- 2 cups kale, chopped
- 1 cup carrots, sliced
- 2 cups fish or vegetable broth

Instructions:

1) Place salmon chunks, kale, carrots, and broth into the slow cooker.
2) Mix gently.
3) Cook on low for 3-4 hours until salmon is cooked through.
4) Allow it to cool before serving.

Nutritional Information:

Calories: 280 | Protein: 25g | Fat: 10g | Carbohydrates: 20g

Tips:

- Kale is a nutrient-dense green, packed with vitamins and minerals.
- Remove salmon skin for easier digestion.

42) Beef and Pumpkin Mash

Cook Time: 4-5 hours on low

Servings: 3-4

Ingredients:

- 1 pound beef stew meat, lean, cubed
- 1 cup pumpkin puree
- 1 cup green beans, chopped
- 3 cups low-sodium beef or vegetable broth

Instructions:

1) Combine beef stew meat, pumpkin puree, green beans, and broth in the slow cooker.
2) Mix thoroughly.
3) Cook on low for 4-5 hours until beef is tender.
4) Allow it to cool before serving.

Nutritional Information:

Calories: 280 | Protein: 25g | Fat: 8g | Carbohydrates: 25g

Tips:

- Pumpkin is gentle on the stomach and provides essential nutrients.
- Choose lean beef to reduce fat content.

43) Chicken and Turmeric Broth

Cook Time: 4-5 hours on low

Servings: 3-4

Ingredients:

- 1 pound boneless, skinless chicken thighs, chopped
- 1 tablespoon turmeric powder
- 2 cups spinach, chopped
- 3 cups low-sodium chicken broth

Instructions:

1) Combine chicken thighs, turmeric powder, spinach, and broth in the slow cooker.
2) Mix gently.
3) Cook on low for 4-5 hours until chicken is tender and flavors meld.
4) Allow it to cool before serving.

Nutritional Information:

Calories: 240 | Protein: 24g | Fat: 8g | Carbohydrates: 10g

Tips:

- Turmeric possesses anti-inflammatory properties.
- Use boneless chicken thighs for easier digestion.

44)   Turkey and Cauliflower Rice Medley

Cook Time: 3-4 hours on low

Servings: 2-3

Ingredients:

- 1 pound ground turkey
- 2 cups cauliflower florets, riced
- 1 cup broccoli, chopped
- 2 cups low-sodium turkey or vegetable broth

Instructions:

1) Brown the ground turkey in a skillet until fully cooked, then drain excess fat.
2) Combine cooked turkey, cauliflower rice, broccoli, and broth in the slow cooker.
3) Mix well.
4) Cook on low for 3-4 hours until vegetables are tender.
5) Allow it to cool before serving.

Nutritional Information:

Calories: 240 | Protein: 22g | Fat: 8g | Carbohydrates: 20g

CHAPTER 6
STORAGE AND SERVING SUGGESTIONS

As you embark on the journey of preparing homemade slow cooker dog food for your beloved pet, it's imperative to understand the crucial aspects of storing these delectable meals, determining appropriate serving sizes, and mastering the art of reheating and freezing. This chapter is dedicated to unraveling the intricacies of storing and serving homemade dog food with utmost care and convenience.

STORAGE OF HOMEMADE DOG FOOD

Ensuring proper storage of homemade dog food is pivotal in maintaining its freshness, nutritional integrity, and safety for your furry friend. Follow these guidelines to store your slow cooker creations effectively:

1. Refrigeration: Allow homemade dog food to cool completely before storing it in airtight containers in the refrigerator. Use shallow containers to facilitate rapid cooling and prevent bacterial growth. Refrigerated homemade dog food can typically stay fresh for up to 3-5 days.

2. Freezing: For longer-term storage, freezing homemade dog food is a convenient option. Portion the food into smaller containers or freezer bags, removing excess air before sealing. Properly frozen homemade dog food can remain safe for consumption for up to 2-3 months.

3. Labeling: Clearly label containers with the date of preparation to keep track of freshness and rotation. Include details of ingredients used if storing multiple recipes to avoid confusion.

4. **Thawing:** When ready to serve frozen homemade dog food, thaw it overnight in the refrigerator or gently heat it using a slow cooker or microwave. Ensure it reaches an appropriate temperature before serving to your pet.

SERVING SIZES AND RECOMMENDATIONS

Determining the right serving size for your furry companion ensures they receive adequate nutrition without overindulging. Consider the following factors when determining serving sizes:

1. **Weight and Activity Level:** Tailor serving sizes based on your dog's weight, age, breed, and activity level. Active dogs may require larger portions, while less active or smaller breeds might need smaller servings to maintain a healthy weight.

2. **Observation**: Monitor your dog's weight, body condition, and energy levels to gauge if the serving sizes are appropriate. Adjust portions as needed to maintain a healthy weight.

3. **Avoid Overfeeding:** Overfeeding can lead to obesity and other health issues. Stick to recommended serving sizes and avoid excessive treats or table scraps.

REHEATING AND FREEZING TIPS

Proper reheating and freezing techniques ensure that every meal served to your furry friend is not just safe but also retains its flavors and nutritional value:

1. Reheating: Thaw frozen homemade dog food in the refrigerator overnight or gently heat it on the stove or in a microwave. Ensure it reaches an appropriate temperature throughout before serving to avoid any potential bacterial growth.

2. Avoid Microwaving Metal Containers: If using metal containers for reheating, transfer the food to a microwave-safe dish before heating. Microwaving metal containers can cause sparks and damage to the microwave.

3. Freezing Tips: When freezing homemade dog food, remove excess air from containers or bags before sealing to prevent freezer burn. Label and date containers for easy identification.

4. Portion Control: Freeze homemade dog food in individual or meal-sized portions for easy thawing and serving without waste.

By mastering the nuances of storing, serving, reheating, and freezing homemade slow cooker dog food, you ensure that every meal served to your furry companion is not just a culinary delight but also a testament to your commitment to their health and happiness.

30 DAY MEAL PLAN

DAY	MEAL	INGREDIENTS	COOK TIME
Day 1	Chicken & Brown Rice Stew	Chicken, Brown Rice, Carrots, Chicken Broth	4-5 hours
Day 2	Turkey & Pumpkin Stew	Ground Turkey, Pumpkin Puree, Green Beans	4-5 hours
Day 3	Salmon & Sweet Potato Mash	Salmon, Sweet Potatoes, Peas, Fish Broth	3-4 hours
Day 4	Beef & Quinoa Delight	Beef Stew Meat, Quinoa, Carrots, Beef Broth	4-5 hours
Day 5	Chicken & Vegetable Broth	Chicken Breast, Green Beans, Carrots, Broth	4-5 hours
Day 6	Bison & Lentil Casserole	Bison Meat, Lentils, Carrots, Vegetable Broth	4-5 hours

SLOW COOKER DOG FOOD COOKBOOK

Day 7	Lamb & Barley Stew	Lamb Stew Meat, Barley, Carrots, Lamb Broth	4-5 hours
Day 8	Duck & Pumpkin Stew	Duck Breast, Pumpkin Puree, Green Peas	3-4 hours
Day 9	Venison & Cranberry Stew	Venison Meat, Cranberries, Potatoes, Broth	4-5 hours
Day 10	Pork & Apple Casserole	Pork Loin, Apples, Sweet Potatoes, Pork Broth	4-5 hours
Day 11	Chicken & Turmeric Broth	Chicken Thighs, Turmeric Powder, Spinach, Broth	4-5 hours
Day 12	Turkey & Cauliflower Rice Medley	Ground Turkey, Cauliflower, Broccoli, Broth	3-4 hours
Day 13	Beef & Pumpkin Mash	Beef Stew Meat, Pumpkin Puree, Green Beans	4-5 hours

SLOW COOKER DOG FOOD COOKBOOK

Day 14	Chicken & Kale Stew	Chicken Breast, Kale, Carrots, Chicken Broth	4-5 hours
Day 15	Salmon & Carrot Casserole	Salmon Fillets, Carrots, Peas, Fish Broth	3-4 hours
Day 16	Beef & Parsnip Stew	Beef Stew Meat, Parsnips, Green Peas, Broth	4-5 hours
Day 17	Turkey & Blueberry Stew	Ground Turkey, Blueberries, Sweet Potatoes	4-5 hours
Day 18	Salmon & Kale Delight	Salmon Fillets, Kale, Carrots, Fish Broth	3-4 hours
Day 19	Beef & Quinoa Medley	Beef Stew Meat, Quinoa, Sweet Potatoes, Broth	4-5 hours
Day 20	Chicken & Zucchini Stew	Chicken Breast, Zucchini, Carrots, Chicken Broth	4-5 hours
Day 21	Lamb & Lentil Casserole	Lamb Shoulder, Lentils, Carrots, Lamb Broth	4-5 hours

SLOW COOKER DOG FOOD COOKBOOK

Day 22	Duck & Broccoli Medley	Duck Breast, Broccoli, Cauliflower, Duck Broth	3-4 hours
Day 23	Venison & Potato Stew	Venison Meat, Potatoes, Green Beans, Broth	4-5 hours
Day 24	Pork & Squash Casserole	Pork Loin, Squash, Apples, Pork Broth	4-5 hours
Day 25	Chicken & Spinach Broth	Chicken Thighs, Spinach, Carrots, Chicken Broth	4-5 hours
Day 26	Turkey & Broccoli Rice Medley	Ground Turkey, Broccoli, Cauliflower, Broth	3-4 hours
Day 27	Beef & Carrot Mash	Beef Stew Meat, Carrots, Peas, Beef Broth	4-5 hours
Day 28	Chicken & Carrot Stew	Chicken Breast, Carrots, Green Beans, Broth	4-5 hours
Day 29	Bison & Sweet Potato Medley	Bison Meat, Sweet Potatoes,	4-5 hours

		Peas, Vegetable Broth	
Day 30	Lamb & Lentil Stew	Lamb Stew Meat, Lentils, Carrots, Lamb Broth	4-5 hours

CONCLUSION

As we reach the end of this culinary journey through the world of slow cooker dog food, I stand in awe of the bond we share—the love for our furry companions and the dedication to their well-being that unites us. Crafting homemade meals for our dogs isn't just about nourishment; it's a testament to the profound connection we have with our loyal friends.

Your dedication to exploring the art of slow cooking for your beloved pets is truly commendable. You've ventured into the realm of wholesome ingredients, culinary creativity, and nutritional excellence, all in the pursuit of providing the best for your furry companions.

I hope the recipes, guidance, and insights shared within these pages have not only tantalized your pet's taste buds but also instilled in you the confidence to embrace the joy of crafting meals that prioritize health, flavor, and love.

Your feedback, thoughts, and experiences matter immensely. I encourage you to share your stories, successes, and even challenges you've encountered while embarking on this flavorful journey. Your input will help not only in refining your culinary endeavors but also in fostering a community dedicated to the well-being of our four-legged friends.

Remember, your commitment to nourishing your dog's body and soul with homemade meals isn't just a choice; it's a celebration—a celebration of love, dedication, and the cherished moments shared with our furry companions.

Thank you for embarking on this culinary adventure with me. Your feedback is invaluable as we strive to continuously improve and create an even more enriching experience for the next leg of this journey.

Let your kitchen be filled with the aroma of love, and your furry friend's heart be filled with the joy of every meticulously crafted meal. Together, let's continue to savor the delight of slow cooker dog cuisine.

SLOW COOKER DOG FOOD COOKBOOK

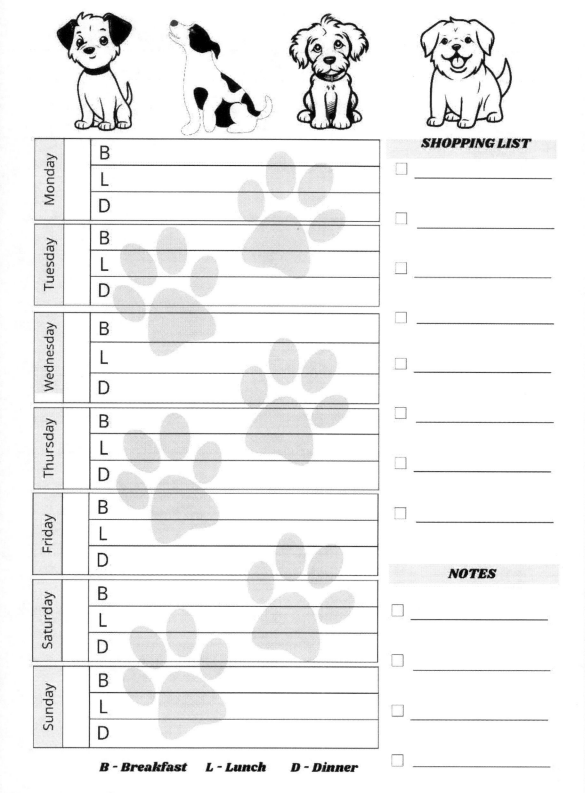

Monday	B	
	L	
	D	
Tuesday	B	
	L	
	D	
Wednesday	B	
	L	
	D	
Thursday	B	
	L	
	D	
Friday	B	
	L	
	D	
Saturday	B	
	L	
	D	
Sunday	B	
	L	
	D	

SHOPPING LIST

☐ _____
☐ _____
☐ _____
☐ _____
☐ _____
☐ _____
☐ _____

NOTES

☐ _____
☐ _____
☐ _____
☐ _____

B - Breakfast   L - Lunch   D - Dinner

SLOW COOKER DOG FOOD COOKBOOK

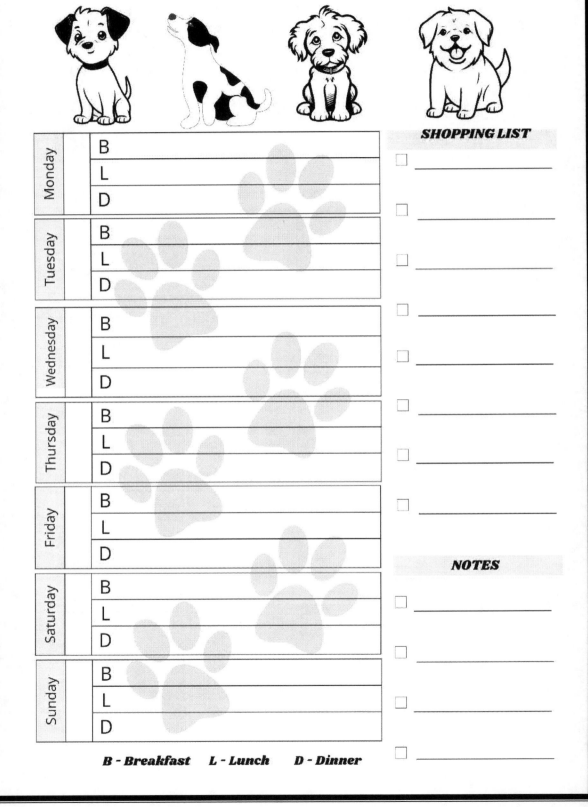

Monday	B	
	L	
	D	
Tuesday	B	
	L	
	D	
Wednesday	B	
	L	
	D	
Thursday	B	
	L	
	D	
Friday	B	
	L	
	D	
Saturday	B	
	L	
	D	
Sunday	B	
	L	
	D	

B - Breakfast   L - Lunch   D - Dinner

SHOPPING LIST

☐ _____

☐ _____

☐ _____

☐ _____

☐ _____

☐ _____

☐ _____

☐ _____

NOTES

☐ _____

☐ _____

☐ _____

☐ _____

SLOW COOKER DOG FOOD COOKBOOK

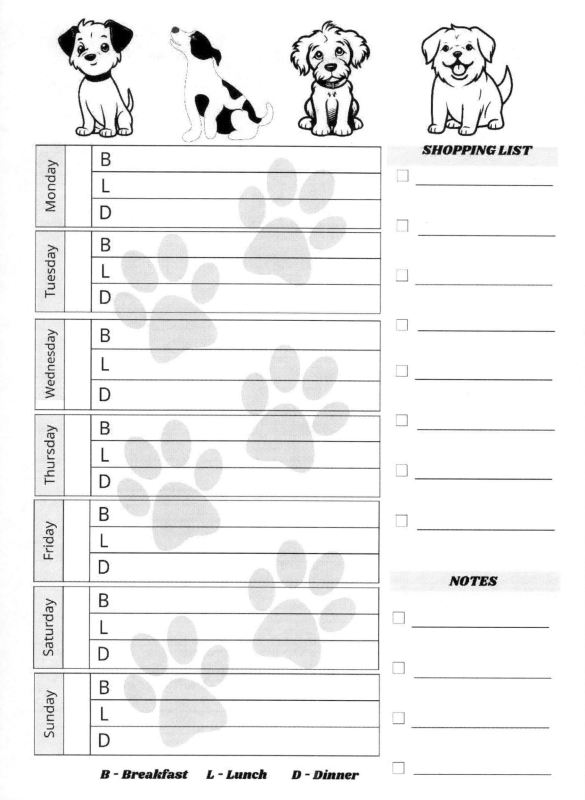

SHOPPING LIST

Monday	B
	L
	D

Tuesday	B
	L
	D

Wednesday	B
	L
	D

Thursday	B
	L
	D

Friday	B
	L
	D

NOTES

Saturday	B
	L
	D

Sunday	B
	L
	D

B - Breakfast   L - Lunch   D - Dinner

SLOW COOKER DOG FOOD COOKBOOK

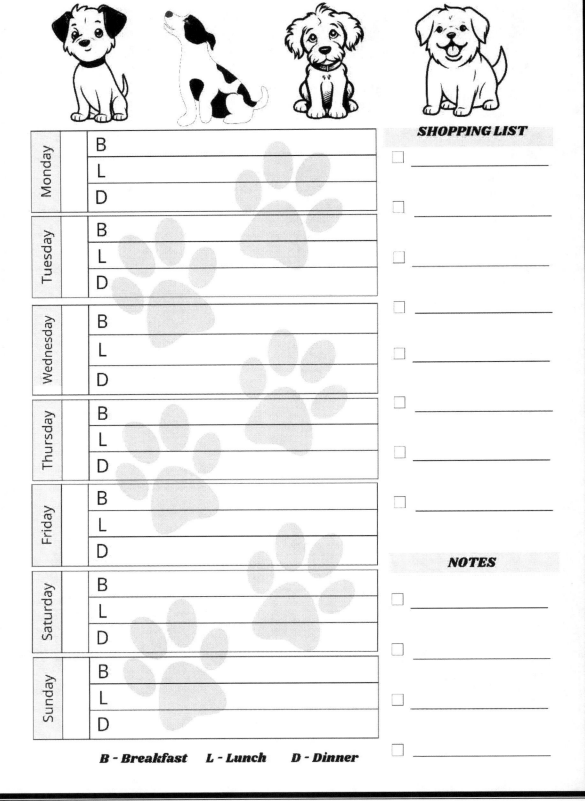

SHOPPING LIST

	Meal	
Monday	B	
	L	
	D	
Tuesday	B	
	L	
	D	
Wednesday	B	
	L	
	D	
Thursday	B	
	L	
	D	
Friday	B	
	L	
	D	
Saturday	B	
	L	
	D	
Sunday	B	
	L	
	D	

NOTES

B - Breakfast   L - Lunch   D - Dinner

SLOW COOKER DOG FOOD COOKBOOK

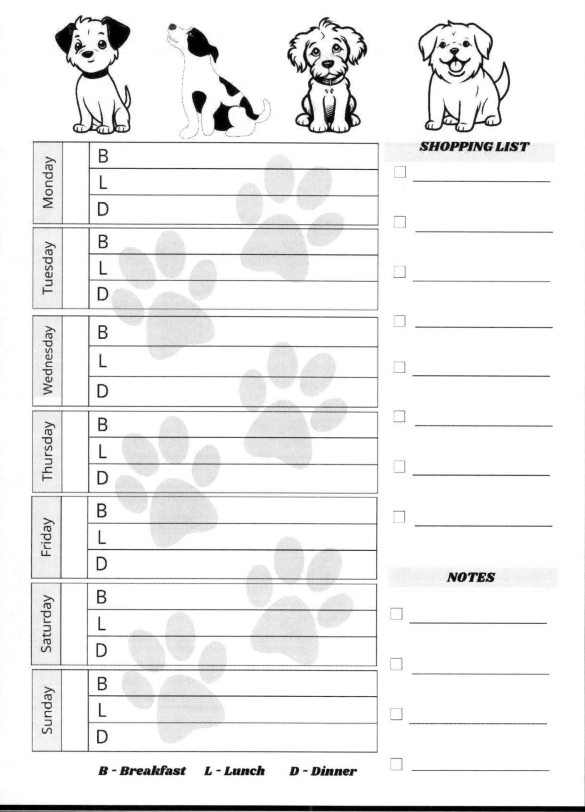

Monday	B	
	L	
	D	
Tuesday	B	
	L	
	D	
Wednesday	B	
	L	
	D	
Thursday	B	
	L	
	D	
Friday	B	
	L	
	D	
Saturday	B	
	L	
	D	
Sunday	B	
	L	
	D	

B - Breakfast   L - Lunch   D - Dinner

SHOPPING LIST

☐ _____

☐ _____

☐ _____

☐ _____

☐ _____

☐ _____

☐ _____

NOTES

☐ _____

☐ _____

☐ _____

☐ _____

SLOW COOKER DOG FOOD COOKBOOK

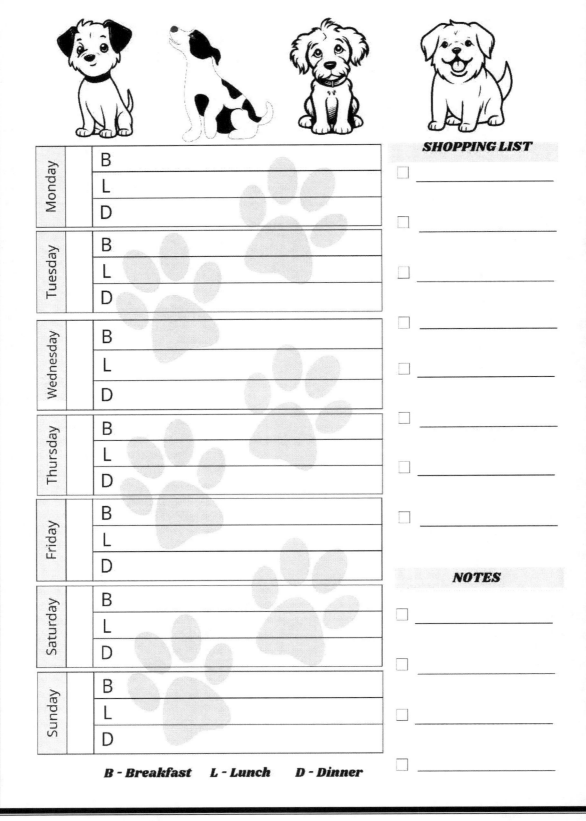

Monday	B
	L
	D

Tuesday	B
	L
	D

Wednesday	B
	L
	D

Thursday	B
	L
	D

Friday	B
	L
	D

Saturday	B
	L
	D

Sunday	B
	L
	D

SHOPPING LIST

☐ _____
☐ _____
☐ _____
☐ _____
☐ _____
☐ _____
☐ _____

NOTES

☐ _____
☐ _____
☐ _____
☐ _____

B - Breakfast   L - Lunch   D - Dinner

SLOW COOKER DOG FOOD COOKBOOK

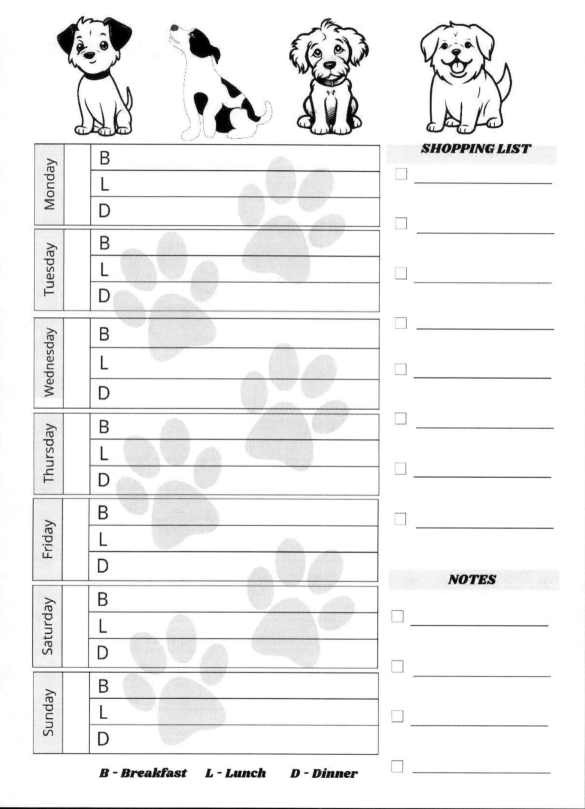

Monday	B	
	L	
	D	
Tuesday	B	
	L	
	D	
Wednesday	B	
	L	
	D	
Thursday	B	
	L	
	D	
Friday	B	
	L	
	D	
Saturday	B	
	L	
	D	
Sunday	B	
	L	
	D	

B - Breakfast   L - Lunch   D - Dinner

SHOPPING LIST

☐ _____
☐ _____
☐ _____
☐ _____
☐ _____
☐ _____
☐ _____

NOTES

☐ _____
☐ _____
☐ _____
☐ _____

SLOW COOKER DOG FOOD COOKBOOK

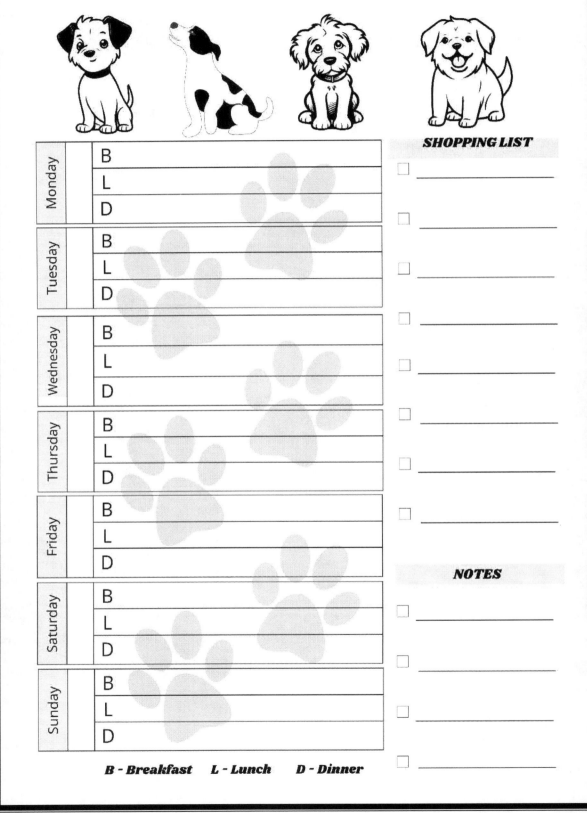

Monday	B	
	L	
	D	
Tuesday	B	
	L	
	D	
Wednesday	B	
	L	
	D	
Thursday	B	
	L	
	D	
Friday	B	
	L	
	D	
Saturday	B	
	L	
	D	
Sunday	B	
	L	
	D	

B - Breakfast   L - Lunch   D - Dinner

SHOPPING LIST

☐ _____
☐ _____
☐ _____
☐ _____
☐ _____
☐ _____
☐ _____

NOTES

☐ _____
☐ _____
☐ _____
☐ _____